S7 are undeniably the hottest pop sensation of the decade. Since their first release back in June 1999, they have notched up a string of number one hits, three hugely successful albums, top rating tv shows and awards far too numerous to name. They proved themselves the world over when in the summer of 2001 they embarked on their first UK tour.

The S Club phenomenon is not only UK, or even Europe, based, the seven are now international stars. Their very first tv series, *Miami 7,* beamed them into homes in 100 countries. Their singles too have made gold and platinum sales around the globe, including Australia, Canada and the US. Of course with this success comes press, publicity, pressure...and merchandise galore! It seems everyone wants a piece of S Club 7. As well as the music, you can buy videos, magazines, books, posters, bags, dolls...you can even create your own t shirt on the S Club 7 website.

Each of the seven has their own unique talent and personality and it's this individuality and strength of character which makes them unique as a whole. Together as S Club 7, the world is their oyster. Read on and discover the secret of the S Club success...

Published by
Grandreams Books Ltd
4 North Parade
Bath BA1 1LF
England

Printed in Italy

contents

The S Club 7 story begins in 1998 when ex-manager of the Spice Girls, Simon Fuller took on a number of talent scouts to search for a new five piece band. The talent spotters went to every theatre school, club and holiday camp across Britain. The audition stages lasted eight months and by the end of 1998, seven, not five as originally planned, excited wannabes were recruited. The first to be taken on were Paul, Jon and Hannah.

Hannah and Paul already knew each together from attending the National Music Youth Theatre. After successfully auditioning for S Club 7, Hannah gave up her A level courses.
Jon too answered the audition call and says, "I went along, but didn't really know much about it." Shortly afterwards, he was the third recruit for a new band.

Rachel's story sounds very much like a case of being in the right place at the right time. She was working in fashion and one day went to meet her brother for lunch. While waiting outside his block, two men approached and asked if she could sing. Rachel replied positively and before she knew it had tried out for S Club 7 and got in!

Bradley was one of the last to join, however he has always been involved in music. "Before S Club 7, I was in a band called Krisp with my sister and cousin and also a rap band, although I wasn't very good at it!" Bradley found his way into S Club 7 by recording some sample tracks and sending them to 19 Management. Bradley sincerely believes his being successful at the S Club audition is proof that, "if you want something bad enough, you have to go for it."

Like Bradley, when Jo met with S Club 7 she had plenty of performing experience. "I've been singing since I was 13. I never had any voice training, I just taught myself, spending hours in my bedroom when I was young." Jo was briefly in a band called Solid HarmoniE, then had a top 40 hit in Germany with 2.4 family. She was singing country and western in a bar alongside Kele Le Rock when she was spotted by a producer and asked to audition for S Club 7. With the seven in place, Paul says they all got on well from the outset, "but we did have to break the ice." Jo recognised early that each of her fellow band members had an individual talent. "Everyone has something they specialise in," she said, "...some are stronger singers, some actors and some dancers." It was time to put this new band to the test and start recording.

Reaching for the charts
June 1999 was a big month for S Club 7. Their very first single was released in Britain. In just six days, the single sold a phenomenal 190,000 copies and unsurprisingly reached the number one spot. What followed was hit after hit from the first album entitled S Club. S Club Party was the

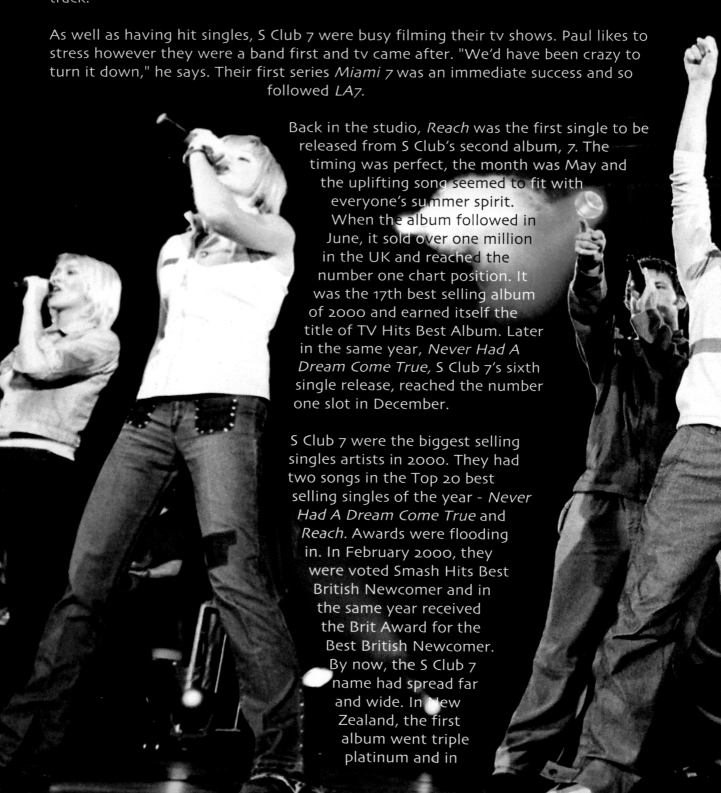

second release which reached the number two chart position in September of '99. S Club 7 were clearly no 'one hit wonder'.

Their debut album, released in October of '99, peaked at number two in the album charts and made double platinum sales status. At the time Jo commented on their rapid success, "I think what we've done is a massive achievement...I remember my mum saying to me when I got in the band, 'just keep your feet on the ground and remember where you come from'. I've stuck to that and I don't think the success has changed me a bit." It is this sound philosophy, which surfaced early in their careers, that has kept the S Clubs on track.

As well as having hit singles, S Club 7 were busy filming their tv shows. Paul likes to stress however they were a band first and tv came after. "We'd have been crazy to turn it down," he says. Their first series *Miami 7* was an immediate success and so followed *LA7*.

Back in the studio, *Reach* was the first single to be released from S Club's second album, *7*. The timing was perfect, the month was May and the uplifting song seemed to fit with everyone's summer spirit. When the album followed in June, it sold over one million in the UK and reached the number one chart position. It was the 17th best selling album of 2000 and earned itself the title of TV Hits Best Album. Later in the same year, *Never Had A Dream Come True,* S Club 7's sixth single release, reached the number one slot in December.

S Club 7 were the biggest selling singles artists in 2000. They had two songs in the Top 20 best selling singles of the year - *Never Had A Dream Come True* and *Reach*. Awards were flooding in. In February 2000, they were voted Smash Hits Best British Newcomer and in the same year received the Brit Award for the Best British Newcomer. By now, the S Club 7 name had spread far and wide. In New Zealand, the first album went triple platinum and in

Chile it took gold status. The tv shows were sold to over 100 countries, making a potential audience of over 90 million.

From the outset, S Club 7 became involved with charities and valuable causes. All the proceeds from *Never Had A Dream Come True* were given to the BBC Children in Need charity. They also support Woolworths Kids First which aims to raise money to support a range of charities for young people. We find out later in the book how each of the seven has worked with the Worldwide Fund For Nature raising awareness of the plight of endangered species.

Non-stop success
After six weeks of rehearsals, 2001 saw S Club 7 taking in a tour of the UK. There were also promotional visits to Canada, Australia, Germany, Sweden, France, Spain and the US. In July they flew to LA to film their third season and a summer special.

The UK summer tour really proved the talent of S Club 7, especially to the cynics who had accused them of not being able to sing! The amazing shows were of a 'musical' style performance with acting, singing and dancing.

When it came to recording S Club's third album, there was a lot more creative input from the seven. "All of us are capable of writing," said Jo at the time, "...so we got a lot more involved." Bradley wrote six new songs, two of which appear on the album. The first single release was in April. The track was *Don't Stop Movin'*. Of course, it was a huge hit...and they keep on coming.

spotlight on: 7

Hannah

Full name: Hannah Louise Spearritt

Nickname(s): Titch, Han, Little Ted

Date of birth: 1st April 1981

Star sign: Aries

Height: 5ft 4"

Colour of hair: Blonde

Colour of eyes: Blue

Distinguishing feature: My smile, so I'm told

Best attribute(s): Being fun and down to earth

Nastiest habit(s): Not being able to sit still, cracking my knuckles

Hometown: Yarmouth

Siblings: Sister Tanya, brother Stuart

First performance: In a local production of Annie when I was 12

Music or tv: I like it all, but being on tv you can sing and dance too

Alternative career(s): Musical theatre, fitness instructor

Favourite album: *Thriller,* Michael Jackson

Favourite food: Sunday roasts

Jon

up close: Jon

You might recognise Jon from appearing in *EastEnders.* He starred as Josh, the boyfriend of Clare, Albert Square resident Nigel's step-daughter. Both have since left the series, so if you missed it, you're not likely to catch Jon on the soap again. He does however look back on his time in 'the Square' with fondness and still keeps in touch with some of the cast, including Natalie Cassidy who plays Sonia . "It was great at the time," Jon says, "but I really missed singing and wanted to do that as well as act."

Wanting more Jon grew up in Devon, but before most of his classmates had completed their first year at secondary school, Jon was acting

14

"i've got the best job being in S Club 7"

on the West End. "I had been taking acting lessons at home and always enjoyed drama at school." He also learnt to play the piano, a skill he's using once again when songwriting with S Club 7. Jon's lucky break came when he successfully auditioned for *Oliver!* Not only did he secure a role in the show, it was the lead.

After the musical's run at the London Palladium, there was no turning back. The Devon countryside held little to offer a young aspiring actor and so Jon enrolled at the Sylvia Young Theatre School in London, the breeding ground for many of today's stars. "I started doing some tv work, including *The Mill on the Floss,* a BBC drama, the *Barrymore Show* and then of course, *EastEnders.*"

Getting personal

Jon describes himself as always up for laugh and a bit of a softie. The S Club he is closest to is Tina and shares a flat with her in LA. Their friendship runs deep, "I'll always stay in touch with Tina whatever happens," he says. When he's not out on the town with his brothers, Jon often goes clubbing with Tina and sometimes Hannah, another party animal. However unlike Hannah, who he says is a nightmare first thing, Jon reckons he's pretty chirpy in the mornings! One of Jon's traits which the S Clubs do find annoying is his sarcasm, "...they never seem to know if I'm serious...sometimes I think I insult people," he admits.

Jon is a vegetarian, extremely health conscious and careful with his appearance. A real fusser with his hair, rumour has it when S Club 7 were last in the States Jon spent his last dollar on a hairbrush! Jon takes sunbathing very seriously but draws the line at using a sunbed for health reasons.

Animal attachments

Jon says since the very outset, he has always missed home when filming in the States with the S Clubs. "Mostly I miss my family and my dog Molly...and of course my mum's cooking...and even the weather sometimes...and the British soaps." It seems there was a time when Jon was particularly attached to Corrie Street, of course these days keeping up with the storylines is near on impossible.

Jon says if he wasn't working as a performer, his chosen career would be with animals. He is an avid supporter of animal causes and so was delighted to become involved in the WWF projects for endangered species. Jon's assignment included trekking through the Malaysian jungle to check out the orangutan. Jon was overawed by the experience, "I never imagined I'd do something like that, I can't describe it...the orangutans are just like humans and really communicate," he enthused.

Full name: Joanne O'Meara

Date of birth: 29th April 1979

Star sign: Taurus

Height: 5ft 4"

Colour of hair: Blonde

Colour of eyes: Blue

Distinguishing feature(s): Numerous tattoos

Nastiest habit(s): Biting my nails, playing with my hair

Hometown: Romford, Essex

Siblings: Sister Julie, brother Shane

Pets: Dog, two cats

First performance: Karaoke, singing *The Locomotion* when I was about 12

First record ever bought: *Postman Pat*

Music or tv: Music

Previous job(s): Checkout girl in a Spar supermarket, working in a pet shop

Favourite food: Chinese

Phobia(s): Tarantulas and cockroaches

Most treasured possession(s): Old teddies Donald and Gus

S Club 7's music success has certainly been matched on screen. *Miami 7* was first aired on BBC1 in April 1999 and became the most watched programme on children's tv. It was scripted by the acclaimed writers of *Friends, Fresh Prince of Bel Air* and *Spiceworld: The Movie*. Most of the series was shot at Lauderdale by the Sea in the US and in the thirteen episodes, we see the seven friends working to entertain guests in a Miami hotel. While filming, the S Clubs stayed at the Paradise Hotel. Many tourists holidaying at the popular destination were lucky enough to get small parts on the shows.

Miami 7 proved an award winning series. It was credited as TV Hits Best Children's TV Show and the Best Disney Channel Show. The feature length specials *Back To The '50s* and *Boyfriends and Birthdays* were also screened in '99 clocking up amazing viewing statistics.

The following year, these successes were followed up with *LA7*, broadcast for 13 weeks in April 2000. The seven are shown this time on the West coast of the US, in LA. Tina found the first episode particularly amusing, "We're performing *I'll Be There* and dressed in all these woolly hats and blankets...it's hilarious." On watching himself in *LA7* Jon comments, "There are some bits where you cringe, but I have to watch to learn from my mistakes." One of his favourite bits of *LA7* was performing Spiritual Love on the beach. He recalls, "The sun was setting in the background and it was a perfect end to a perfect day."

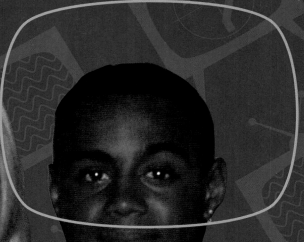

LA schedule

Filming in LA takes up a fair part of the S Club 7 yearly schedule. Jon says it's not performing for the camera which is the hard part, but the hours and hours it takes to record the show. The early mornings shooting schedules certainly aren't popular with night owl Bradley. "We had months of 5.30am wake up calls, I could have dropped!" he says.

Bradley reckons he's the best at acting, although he's not too hot at learning his lines. Paul however takes his acting very seriously as he wants to continue with it in the future. With regards to the scripts, the S Clubs say they are allowed some input. According to Hannah, if they don't like a line, they will say and get it changed. Paul explained how they come up with little bits "to make it more appealing...well hopefully."

Hannah says her character on the show is a massive exaggeration of her own personality. "I'm really not that dippy...but I guess I do do stupid stuff sometimes, but then everyone does." In the shows, undoubtedly Hannah is the biggest flirt. That too she says is an exaggeration. "I was a bit of a flirt in my 16 year old days," she says, "but I don't think I am as much now." Tina reckons her character is much more bossy than she is in real life and as for Rachel, hers is too sensitive. Jo's

ON SCREEN

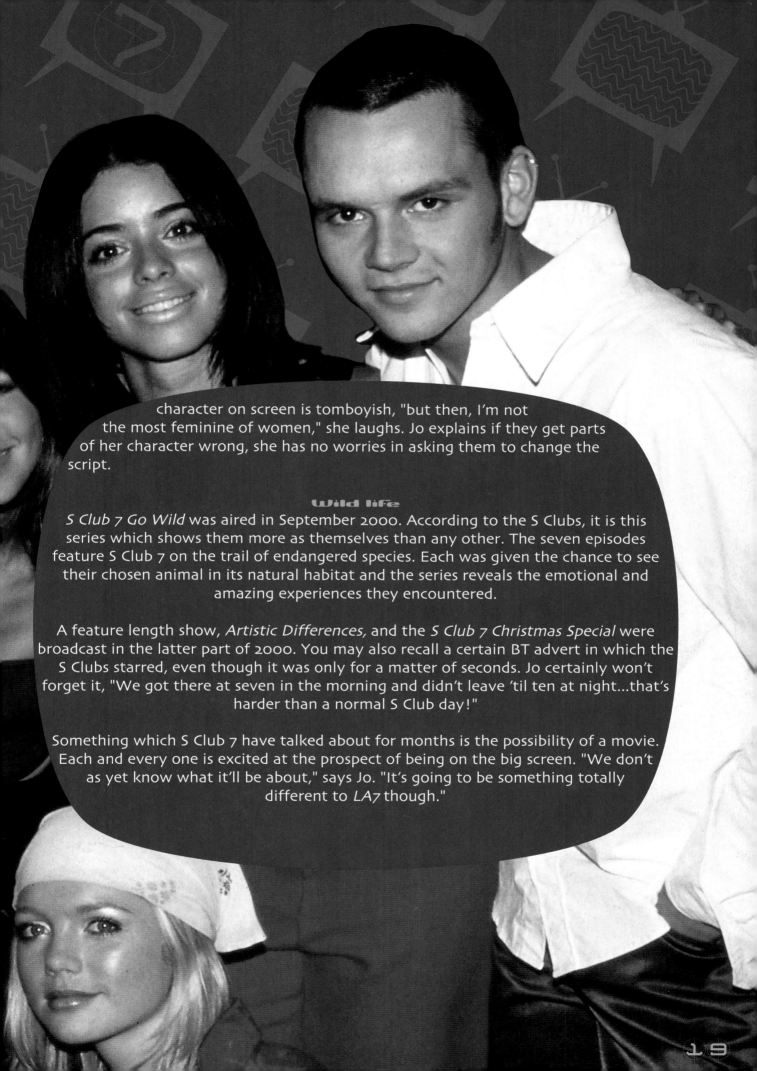

character on screen is tomboyish, "but then, I'm not the most feminine of women," she laughs. Jo explains if they get parts of her character wrong, she has no worries in asking them to change the script.

Wild life

S Club 7 Go Wild was aired in September 2000. According to the S Clubs, it is this series which shows them more as themselves than any other. The seven episodes feature S Club 7 on the trail of endangered species. Each was given the chance to see their chosen animal in its natural habitat and the series reveals the emotional and amazing experiences they encountered.

A feature length show, *Artistic Differences,* and the *S Club 7 Christmas Special* were broadcast in the latter part of 2000. You may also recall a certain BT advert in which the S Clubs starred, even though it was only for a matter of seconds. Jo certainly won't forget it, "We got there at seven in the morning and didn't leave 'til ten at night...that's harder than a normal S Club day!"

Something which S Club 7 have talked about for months is the possibility of a movie. Each and every one is excited at the prospect of being on the big screen. "We don't as yet know what it'll be about," says Jo. "It's going to be something totally different to *LA7* though."

up close: Paul

Paul Cattermole could quite easily have landed a job in complete contrast to being a pop star. His grandfather was a physicist and Paul apparently showed signs of following in his footsteps... or so his teachers at school thought. Paul also showed signs of being a talented rugby player. "I won a competition in the Daily Mail to train with the England squad...unfortunately I wasn't really good enough to do it professionally," he says.

Third time lucky

Having stretched his mind and his body, Paul turned to his artistic side and found love...in the performing arts. The first acting role he took was in *West Side Story* when he was fourteen. "I remember thinking how lucky I was to get the part...I was really nervous, but enjoyed it so much I knew it was what I wanted to do for a living."

Despite being mocked, ambitious young Paul took up dance classes to prepare for a future in musical theatre. He studied at the prestigious Mountview Drama School in London and also joined the National Youth Music Theatre. Here he found himself on stage in a production of Pendragon with a cute young girl named Hannah Spearritt. Little did either of the starry eyed hopefuls know then they would be performing together again in front of fan filled stadiums.

The other S Clubs say Paul is mad about music and all types. His recent favourites include David Grey and Travis. Before he joined the band, Paul played with a rock orientated outfit. "I wouldn't want to go back, even though it was good at the time, I've done the rock star bit," he muses.

On S Club 7's second album, Paul sings main vocals on the track *Love Train,* "I really enjoy singing it even though it's a bit too high for me. You can't help but dance along." Clearly for the S Clubs, the most popular track on 7 is *Reach.* "It's so happy and lively and really popy," says

Paul of his favourite. Paul has said he would love to write an album of his own, but for now is happy having contributed to S Club's third album and, in a solo project, recorded a dance track with Lucid.

Life on the road

Performing live is one of the best parts of being in the band for Paul, "...that's really what I joined S Club 7 for," he says. Paul says another of the best things (and at the same time one of the worst) is that being with S Club is like being in a gang. He likes the fact that there's safety in numbers and there's always a buzz, but on the same account, even a live wire like Paul likes a bit of peace and quiet sometimes...and with S Club, that's hard to find!

When S Club 7 are touring, it's Paul who wins the award for being the worst at getting up in the morning, "I've got three alarm clocks and that's not enough!" he says. Despite enjoying a frantic working and social life, Paul says he does miss home comforts when the S Clubs are away for long periods. "When we were in Miami filming, I missed my family and friends such a lot...I even missed the rain of back home."

Paul is extremely serious about his acting. He says given the choice, and if he was on his own, he would chose acting over a music career. Given the time S Club 7 are no more, Paul would like to further his career in theatre, perhaps even writing a play for the West End. "I'd like to do the lot myself," he says, "...the music, the script and of course act in it as well."

21

Spotlight on:

7

Bradley

Full name: Bradley McIntosh

Nickname(s): Brad, Tosh

Date of birth: 8th August 1981

Star sign: Leo

Height: 5ft 6"

Colour of hair: Black

Colour of eyes: Brown

Best attribute(s): Being cool and smooth

Nastiest habit(s): Being late, snoozing at every given moment

Siblings: Sister

Pets: A cat, Sophie

First performance: In front of the mirror singing and dancing to Michael Jackson

Music or tv: Music, that's what counts to me

Alternative career: None, I always just wanted to be a singer

Most treasured possession(s): Family, mobile phone, CD collection

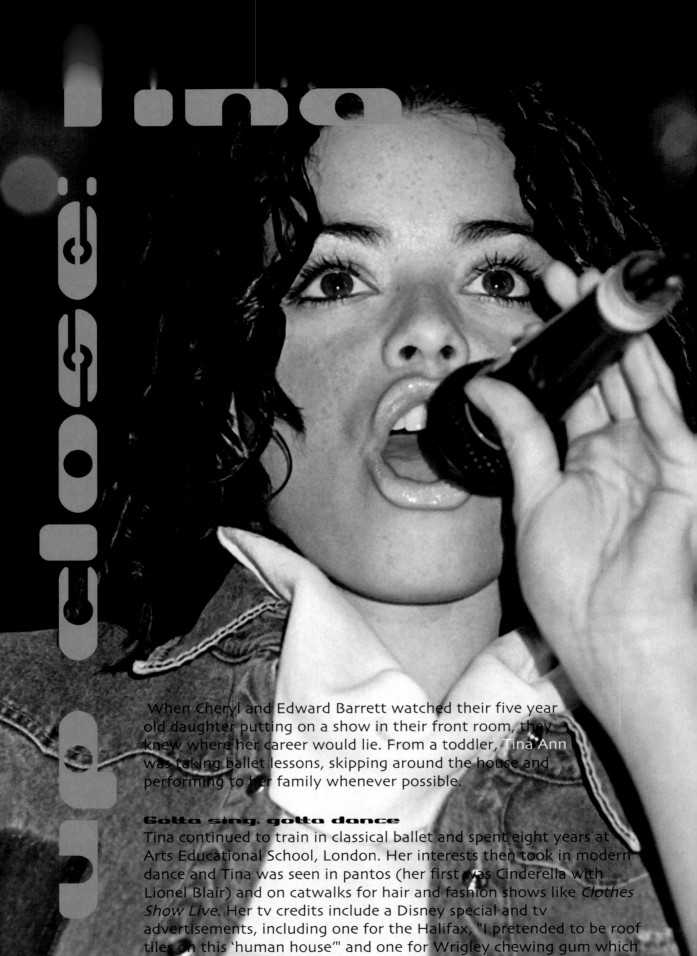

When Cheryl and Edward Barrett watched their five year old daughter putting on a show in their front room, they knew where her career would lie. From a toddler, Tina Ann was taking ballet lessons, skipping around the house and performing to her family whenever possible.

Gotta sing, gotta dance

Tina continued to train in classical ballet and spent eight years at Arts Educational School, London. Her interests then took in modern dance and Tina was seen in pantos (her first was Cinderella with Lionel Blair) and on catwalks for hair and fashion shows like *Clothes Show Live*. Her tv credits include a Disney special and tv advertisements, including one for the Halifax, "I pretended to be roof tiles on this 'human house'" and one for Wrigley chewing gum which was particularly memorable. "It was freezing, I had to wear a bikini and stand in a swimming pool, even between takes all we could wear were these flimsy robes."

Tina's talent for dance paved the way for appearances on *Top of the Pops* before S Club 7 were even thought of. She has danced with lots of groups and artists, including Shola Ama, Toni Braxton and Pulp.

Once Tina became involved with S Club 7, she used her dancing talents to co-choreograph their debut single. Of course, she was thrilled to find they had produced a number one hit. Tina particularly enjoys working on dance routines with choreographers, but points out the S Clubs are sensible and use routines which accommodate everyone's dance levels, ensuring they perform as one. "It would look really odd if I did something completely different to the others just because I've had training," she explains.

For Tina, getting to sing the lead vocals for the first time on I'll Be There was a special moment and one she is quite rightly proud of. "I was really excited and the song seemed to suit my voice...I do these breathy vocals and it actually sounds quite sexy!"

Honest causes
The eldest S Club, Tina is far from bossy. "I don't think anyone could boss them all around!" she laughs. Jon says she is a good listener and expresses his faith in her loyalty, "I could talk to Tina about anything and know she won't tell anyone." Tina is a straight talker and says she doesn't pull any punches. Because of this, rather than the fact she is the oldest, the other S Clubs often come to her for advice. However, Tina does say she can't resist a spot of sarcasm sometimes. "I've probably

offended one or two people in my time!" she admits.

Straight talking Tina put the facts directly to the viewers of *S Club 7 Go Wild!* when she visited China with the WWF to see the world's rarest creature, the giant panda. "By cutting down their bamboo habitat, we are making them starve. (The panda needs to eat for up to 14 hours a day). They will become extinct if we neglect them and disrespect their space," she said. The issue is one close to Tina's heart and being at the actual site with the endangered species made it all the more real for her.

Back in the UK, Tina spoke for all the S Clubs when she said a big thank you to all the fans for the letters and gifts they send. She also explained how unfortunately there is not enough time to reply to each and every one as they get in excess of 100 parcels a week.

So, where lies Tina's future? Despite a traditional training in dance, it is clear she loves all aspects of performing with S Club 7, on stage and on tv. For her to have to chose between the two is a decision she says is just too hard to make.

CLUBBERS'

How much do you really know about S Club 7? Brave the Clubbers' Challenge and find out just how good a fan you really are. Answers can be found on the opposite page...but no cheating!

1. When did the S Clubs first meet?

2. Who once worked with Lionel Blair?

3. Which one of the boys took dance classes when he was younger?

4. Who worked in a shoe shop for their Saturday job?

5. What is the S Club's favourite tv show?

6. Which one of the S Clubs is most religious?

7. Who once said they would like to work with George Michael?

8. Jo admits she is sometimes superstitious, what is the one thing she'll never do?

9. Who worked in Chessington World of Adventures?

10. Jon is a huge fan of which female singer?

11. What is the name of S Club's manager?

12. What is Rachel's favourite song on 7?

13. Who raps in *All In Love Is Fair*?

14. Jo has a very annoying habit, what is it?

15. Getting ready to go out, who is the fussiest about their hair?

16. What does Jon say is his favourite type of song to sing?

17. Who's hero was Danny Kaye?

18. What was the first record Jo ever got?

19. Who would Bradley like to do a duet with?

20. How many tattoos does Jo have?

To join the S Club 7 fan club, write to:
S Club 7
Freepost CV744
3 Alveston Place
Leamington Spa
CV32 4BR

To find S Club on the web, visit:
www.sclub7.com

Answers: 1. 1998. 2. Tina, in a pantomime. 3. Paul, "I got laughed at a lot!" 4. Rachel. "I never actually had to put the shoes on the customer's feet though...I didn't fancy the idea of that." 5. *Friends*. 6. Bradley. 7. Rachel. 8. Walk under a ladder. 9. Bradley, hardly a glamourous role though...in the pizza Hut! 10. Celine Dion. "I think she's fantastic!" 11. Simon Fuller. 12. *Natural*, "...one of the main reasons of course is because I get to sing the main vocals on it", 13. Bradley, although originally it was going to be Jo. 14. She picks her eyelashes when she's tired. 15. Jon. 16. Ballads. 17. Paul's. 18. *Postman Pat!* 19. Stevie Wonder. 20. Five.

spotlight on 7

Rachel

Full name: Rachel Lauren Stevens

Nickname(s): Rach, Ratz

Date of birth: 9th April 1978

Star sign: Aries

Height: 5ft 3"

Colour of hair: Brown

Colour of eyes: Dark brown

Distinguishing feature(s): Belly button piercing, iron burn on right wrist

Best attribute: Ambition

Nastiest habit(s): Clocking up a massive phone bill, chewing gum

Siblings: Brothers Jason and Leigh

Pets: Dog, Rocky

Training: London School of Fashion

First performance: A play with my Saturday drama school

Music or tv: Music, although I would like to do a film

Alternative career: Fashion PR

Favourite album: Ladies and Gentlemen, George Michael

Favourite food: Chinese

Phobia: Getting stuck in a lift

Most treasured possession: I couldn't live without my mobile!

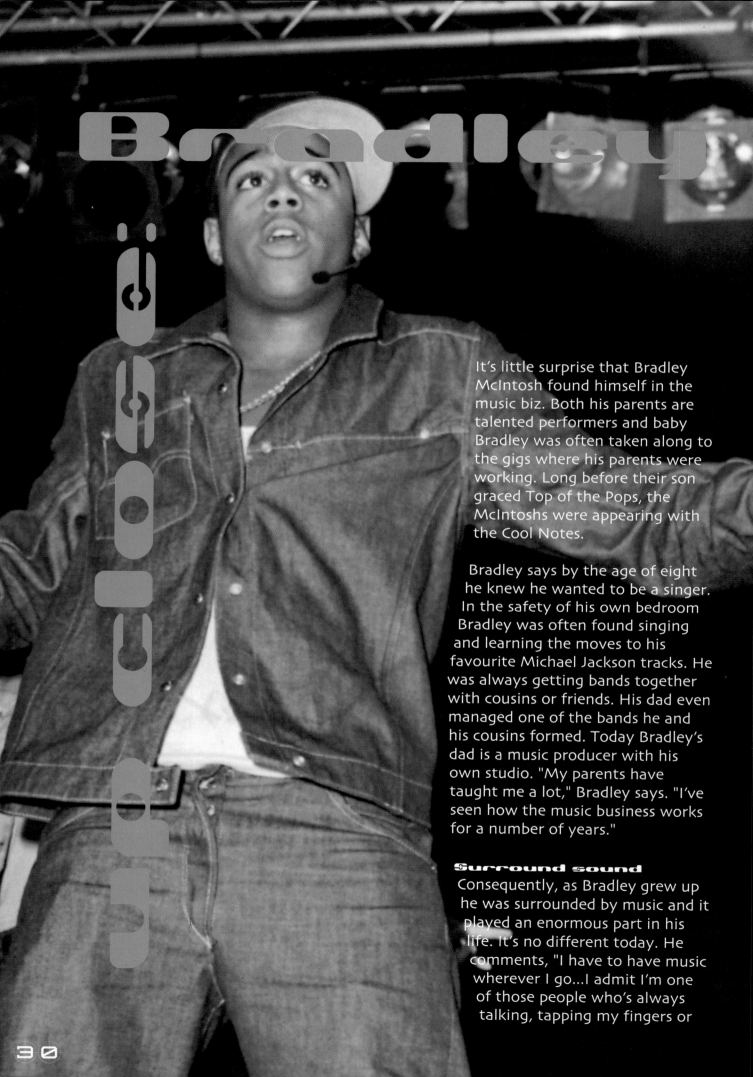

Bradley

up close

It's little surprise that Bradley McIntosh found himself in the music biz. Both his parents are talented performers and baby Bradley was often taken along to the gigs where his parents were working. Long before their son graced Top of the Pops, the McIntoshs were appearing with the Cool Notes.

Bradley says by the age of eight he knew he wanted to be a singer. In the safety of his own bedroom Bradley was often found singing and learning the moves to his favourite Michael Jackson tracks. He was always getting bands together with cousins or friends. His dad even managed one of the bands he and his cousins formed. Today Bradley's dad is a music producer with his own studio. "My parents have taught me a lot," Bradley says. "I've seen how the music business works for a number of years."

Surround sound
Consequently, as Bradley grew up he was surrounded by music and it played an enormous part in his life. It's no different today. He comments, "I have to have music wherever I go...I admit I'm one of those people who's always talking, tapping my fingers or

humming." He always carries a small collection of favourite cds with him, even when S Club are touring.

It was Bradley who suggested his singing the Stevie Wonder track for the 7 album. Initially the others were doubtful, unsure they could do the song justice. However as Paul says, "Once we heard Bradley sing it, we changed our minds...it really is a fantastic version of a brilliant song." Bradley was overwhelmed at covering a song by one of his heros, Stevie Wonder, who he calls, "a real genius". Another cover which Bradley names as a favourite on 7 is *Spiritual Love*, originally recorded by Urban Species.

On this second album, Bradley was the first of the S Clubs to get involved with the writing process. He worked with the S Club songwriters Tim and Stephen on *Best Friend*. Bradley recalls, "I started singing the tune and worked on the lyrics and they added their ideas." Bradley apparently took inspiration for the song from his younger days of hanging out with his mates.

Bird watching

If it's not Bradley's music playing, it's his mobile phone ringing! Having firmly established himself as S Club's 'ladeez man', Bradley keeps his mobile at the ready should anyone 'important' call!

You could say girls are at the forefront of Bradley's mind, despite protestations that he's calmed down a lot. Once asked about his favourite time of year, he responded, "Summer of course, when all the girls come out wearing less!" One of Bradley's dream ladies is Mariah Carey.

Blagging about his experience in bird watching, Bradley spent time with the WWF on the trail of the rare Hyacinth macaw parrot in Brazil. "Seeing the parrots in the rainforest where they belong, they look so beautiful," he said in a rare serious moment. "...but because so many are captured and sold as pets and their habitats are being destroyed, they are nearing extinction," he added. Bradley found out from experts there are in fact only 3000 of the species left in Brazil.

Night owl

Birds aside, Bradley's also renowned for falling asleep (hardly a turn on for the girls!). "The others reckon I could probably fall asleep anywhere," he says. It sounds pretty much true. Apparently Brad has fallen asleep under a table, during breakfast and even while filming while locked in a car boot!

When he's finally awake, which is usually later than sooner, ("You can't get him out of bed in the mornings and you can't get him to bed at night," says Jo), Bradley is pretty hyper, another trait from his childhood. "At school I was quite hyperactive. The teachers didn't really like me, but we still had a laugh with them. I was a bit disruptive in class I suppose, a bit of a class clown." In weak defence, he adds, "But I was always trying to entertain. I'd liven up a boring class by doing something stupid!" Apparently the lessons Bradley most enjoyed were graphic design and PE, "cos you could mess around"...no surprise there then!

It's hard to imagine a Bradley without a smile on his face, but very occasionally he does get stressed with the hectic S Club lifestyle. "It's hard when you don't get a minute to yourself," he says, "But I always do try and smile though."

Spotlight on: Jon

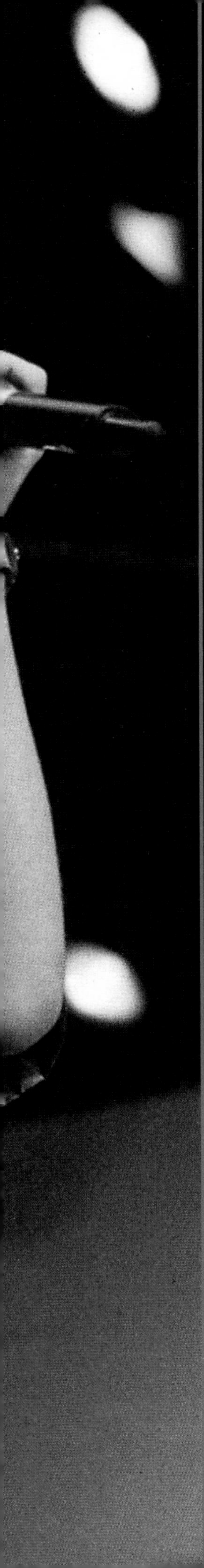

Full name: Jon Lee

Nickname: Jonny Boy

Date of birth: 26th April 1982

Star sign: Taurus

Height: 5ft 7"

Colour of hair: Blonde

Colour of eyes: Brown

Distinguishing feature(s): Two tattoos

Best attribute: Making people laugh

Nastiest habit(s): Biting toenails, being sarcastic

Home: Devon

Siblings: Brothers Jamie and Ben, sister Cassie

Pets: Dog Molly, guinea pigs Charlie Brown and Barney, budgie Harry Boy, fish - lots of!

Training: Sylvia Young Theatre School, London

First performance: Age four in a play at school in Devon

Music or tv: Music, without a doubt

Alternative career: Working with animals

Favourite film: *Clash of the Titans*

Favourite tv show: *Big Brother*

Favourite food: Roast chicken

hannah

spers'i

Bubbly Hannah feels most at ease in the limelight, after all she's been in front of the camera since she was three. The assignment for Mothercare was the first of many modelling jobs as a child.

At school in Great Yarmouth, Hannah was known for two things - flirting and talking too much.
"When I was little I was a terrible flirt, I loved boys...at primary school we used to share boyfriends and swap all the time. The boys would line up behind the bikesheds for kisses."

Centre court to centre stage

When she wasn't making eyes at the boys, Hannah

excelled at sports, particularly tennis, swimming and running. In fact, one of her career plans was to become a professional tennis player. "I used to watch Wimbledon every year and dream of being on centre court," she says.

All that changed however when she took to the stage in Annie with a local theatre company. It was then, at the age of 12, Hannah made up her mind she was to become a performer. A natural on stage, she proved her talent in musical theatre and took roles in the National Youth Music Theatre's production of Pendragon, where she first met Paul, and Bugsy Malone in the West End.

Hannah also made appearances on tv in *Blue Peter*, *The National Lottery Show* and an advertisement for Mercedes. In 1998, she starred in the BBC film *The Cater Street Hangman*, one of her biggest early screen roles.

Pop transition

The transition from musical theatre and tv to pop came naturally for Hannah. She says she enjoys the S Club 7 sound despite the fact that the band have been slated for not being a 'proper band' (whatever that is). "We appeal to a certain market...we create music and perform it...all bands are different." Hannah says one of her favourite tracks on *7* is *Stand By You*, the number on which she and Tina sing lead vocals. "It's a top pop song," she grins.

Nowadays, Hannah shares a flat with mates Sheridan and Neil and considers herself pretty happy go lucky and down to earth. Ever the live wire, Hannah spends her spare time relaxing in pursuits like go-karting or skiing (relaxing?). When she went to Brazil on the trail of the Macaw parrot with Bradley, Hannah managed to fit in a spot of hang-gliding. "I did it off a huge mountain, it was a bit scarey...but I ended up doing it twice!" Paul says of Hannah, "She is a bit hyper at times and she'll always liven things up when we get together."

It's hard to imagine chirpy Hannah falling out with anyone, let alone her fellow band members, but it has been known to happen. "We do have rows, but that's inevitable because we spend so much time together, it gets to you....Most of the time we just have a good laugh though," she says.

Hannah finds it hard to imagine life without the band. However, should she need to find an alternative career path, Hannah says she'd love to go back to the theatre and perhaps appear in a West End show.

spotlight

7

Full name: Tina Ann Barrett

Nickname(s): Tina Bell, Teeny, Teen

Date of birth: 16th September 1976

Star sign: Virgo

Height: 5ft 6"

Colour of hair: Dark brown

Colour of eyes: Brown

Distinguishing feature(s): Huge chocolate brown eyes

Best attribute(s): Independence, being a straight talker

Nastiest habit: Being sarcastic

Pets: None, I used to have a cat

Training: Classical ballet, then Arts Educational School, London

First performance: Dancing show

Music or tv: I really couldn't choose between the two

Alternative career(s): Presenting tv, dancing

Favourite food: Italian

Loved Up

They're one of the most talked about young bands in pop. Everyone wants to know the intimate details of their personal lives. Speculation runs high on who's seeing who and if there is any romance within the band. We take a look at some S Club 7 secrets and how the seven really rate in the romance stakes.

An early start

It seems the S Clubs aren't short of experience when it comes down to romance, especially the boys. They certainly started young. Bradley boasts that at the age of 12, he used to go to discos and would join in competitions to snog as many girls as possible in the night! "The most I snogged was 12," he grins. Jon wasn't far behind, he was up to just the same at his local youth club and once got 12 Valentine cards from 12 different girls! Paul too was a hit with the girls even at primary school where he admits he was seeing two girls at once.

Not to let the girls side down, Hannah is a self confessed flirt, at least she was when she was younger and admits she has been caught out mid snog on a number of occasions, "...behind the bike sheds, in the loo..." apparently in a cupboard once on a school trip! Nowadays however, Hannah's far too busy and reckons she can't really be bothered. "For me to be in a relationship, it has to be really, really good," she says.

Brotherly love

There have been countless rumours about the S Clubs dating each other. One such story came out about Jo and Bradley, it was a complete lie and one Jo actually found quite amusing. There was another about Tina and Jon. Jo likes to put the lid on any such stories. "We're too much like brothers and sisters...None of us fancy each other, it's just not like that," she says. However, she does think all the boys quite handsome, but as for fancying one herself, they're not really her type. Jo likes a short, scruffy, jeans kind of guy. She says the most important thing in life is love and proved this when she got engaged at the end of 2000 to her long term boyfriend Lee. Jo has never professed to be a romantic and wouldn't have appreciated a slushy proposal, "I'm certainly not into all that...I'd kick him out!"

All of the S Clubs have at some time expressed regret at how difficult it is to maintain a relationship while in S Club 7. For Jon, "It's because we're away so much...we never seem to be anywhere for more than a few days." Rachel too says it's the travel abroad and physically getting to see someone. When she split with her long term boyfriend in early 2001, she said it was inevitable as the time was right, even if she hadn't have been in S Club 7. Asked if she would give up the band for a man, Hannah says there would be no way. "I'm still young, I wouldn't want to give it up. I don't think I'm being selfish, I'm just not ready to settle yet."

Guys for girls

So what kind of men do Hannah, Jo, Rachel and Tina go for? Luckily, they don't have the same tastes in men. Rachel has said she likes a man with a nice tan, a great back and nice aftershave! Apparently though she's never had the guts to ask a guy out. According to Jo, Tina is a fan of men in uniforms. "I don't like really clean cut men," Tina says, "...and I can't stand men who go to a club and just want to sit down, they're so boring." She's not into weedy men either and likes a man with strong arms...apparently

Johnny Depp would do nicely!

Hannah is a big fan of Leonardo de Caprio and Brad Pitt. Spending so much time in LA however hasn't endeared her to the all-American look. Hannah says she likes a guy with "a great bod" and a sense of humour. Apparently, making Hannah laugh is all important, even more so than looks.

Girls for guys

Rachel reckons the boys get far more attention from the fans, "but then I think the female fans are much more fanatical." Jo says that the older women tend to go for Paul, the younger girls for Jon and as for Bradley, "well, he attracts everyone...but I know him and he's not that cute!"

Bradley knows he's renowned as the S Club Romeo and defends himself with pleas that he's not as bad as he used to be! "I do respect women, but I'm young, free and happy at the moment. I'd only get in a relationship if I thought she's the one." And once he found her? "If it was good, it's got to be worth staying with...so I would be true to it." The S Clubs say Bradley is a great one for chat up lines and Paul says the only time Bradley looses his cool is when a woman walks by!

Jon likes a girl with a nice smile and one with 'good body language', one perhaps like actress Minnie Driver.

Paul has high aspirations. His ideal woman is Elle McPherson. Though he has been in love before, Paul says right now he is enjoying being free and single. He reckons American girls and British girls are very different. "The LA girls are really up front. If they like you, they'll come and say so...wherever it is." But don't fear, the word is, the S Club boys definitely prefer British girls.

close up on Jo

Jo has been described as 'a top bloke' (Paul), 'generous, loud and easy to get on with' (Hannah) and, by self analysis, 'quiet as a mouse'. Yes, there's many sides to Jo O'Meara, lead vocalist on most of S Club 7's hits.

"I can be mad and full on one moment and then the next I'll be quiet and won't say a thing," Jo admits. She's a great mix of being fun-loving and sensible. Jo's always up for a party, but usually first to get off to bed, well aware she can be a little grumpy in the mornings!

Before Jo joined S Club 7, she was performing in clubs up and down the country. It may come as a surprise, but Jo was known for her Country & Western singing. "It's not the traditional stuff I like, but the 'New Country' like Shania Twain and LeAnn Rimes," she explains. Jo is no stranger to tv either. Before S Club, she appeared on tv singing and even had a top 40 hit in Germany.

Karaoke queen
Despite Jo's first musical interest being in the Postman Pat song, she has come a long way since dancing in her bedroom to Michael Jackson.

"Being in S Club 7 is the business"

"He's been my idol since I was about five, he's such a genius," she says.

It was Jo's father who initially noticed her talent and encouraged her to take to the stage. Her debut was singing *The Locomotion* on karaoke when she was just twelve. Her dad Dave then encouraged her to sing more and more during the family evening out. "I loved the applause and all the attention and so stayed up there singing my heart out!" Jo became something of a karaoke queen in her hometown of Romford in Essex. She still can't resist it today. "I just love karaoke," she says, "The only problem is when someone winds me up and puts on S Club 7 songs."

Jo spent a few terms at the Italia Conti Stage School in London and to subsidise her singing jobs took on a number of not so glamorous part-time jobs. These included being a checkout girl at Spar supermarket, waitressing and working in a pet shop which she says she really enjoyed, "until one day when I found a dog which was dead. It was so upsetting, I had to leave after that."

Animal lover

Jo is a true animal lover. When she was at home, the family had three horses and Jo was dedicated in looking after them. She was of course excited and thrilled to be part of the WWF's campaign for endangered species. Jo chose the Asian elephant to support and went on a trek with the WWF through Thailand on the trail of the animal to make the *S Club 7 Go Wild!* series. She spoke of her experiences, "I've always loved the elephant but was really nervous...I didn't know what to expect. When I was there staring the elephants in the face, I feel I became a changed person." The Asian elephants are in fact in danger because of illegal poaching and the disappearance of their natural habitat due to deforestation. On learning there are now only 50,000 left in the wild, Jo said shortly after filming, "We must help keep them alive...I certainly fell in love with them and hope the viewers did too."

Life in the fast lane

Ask Jo which is her favourite track on 7 and there is no hesitation. "It has to be *Reach*. I love the song...it's really uplifting, like a shot of energy. In fact, I often get the giggles when we perform this one because it makes me feel so good!"

Despite loving the buzz of performing, Jo is quick to emphasise how much hard work is involved with S Club 7. "I get overtired and a bit grumpy when we've been on the go for weeks on end. I just have to remind the others not to push it!" she laughs. To Jo, having time off is a real luxury and she says in long breaks, like Christmas, all she really wants to do is catch up with her folks. "I'm quite family orientated and so when we get a break, I love just being around my family and Lee."

Straight talking, generous and a softie at heart, Jo is of course engaged to Lee. "I can't wait to be married, I'm well up for kids as well...but not just yet!"

spotlight on

paul

7

Full name: Paul Cattermole

Nickname(s): Gwaks, Guacamole, Cat

Date of birth: 7th March 1977

Star sign: Pisces

Height: 5ft 9"

Colour of hair: Brown

Colour of eyes: Brown

Distinguishing feature(s): Ring in left nipple, smelly feet

Best attribute: Enthusiasm

Nastiest habit(s): Snipping toenails and watching them fly across the room, being untidy

Siblings: Sister Treena, brothers Colin and Martin

Training: Mountview Drama School, London

First performance: In a local theatre production of *West Side Story*

Music or tv: Tough choice, if I was on my own, I'd probably choose to act

Alternative career: My teachers at school wanted me to become a physicist

Most treasured possession: A family heirloom - a Hunter watch

up close:

Rachel Lauren was born to the Stevens family in April of 1978. Recognising the early signs of talent, Mum Linda and Dad Michael were soon taking their five year old daughter to drama school every Saturday.

fashion first

It was to be some time however before Rachel started her music career. On leaving school, she chose to take up fashion and studied at the London School of Fashion. Rachel then worked in the public relations area of the business until the call came for S Club 7 in 1998.

Rachel is petite and stands at just 5ft 3" (she has been known to say she wishes she had longer legs). Her stunning looks were noticed at an early age. While she was still at school, Rachel won a J17 hair modelling competition and from this gained a few modelling jobs. Modest as ever, Rachel says, "I really didn't expect to win."

More recently, Rachel has appeared on the cover of men's magazine, *FHM*. With the other S Club girls, a photo shoot took place on a luxurious boat and according to Rachel, who was quite at ease in the spotlight, it felt more like a holiday.

friends and family

So what's Rachel really like? We know she's a bit of a shopaholic, especially when there is the temptation of the designer shops in LA. She also admits to being a bit fussy and quite sensible, "but not too sensible." Rachel always carries her personal organiser. Another thing which travels everywhere with Rachel is her photo album full of piccies of friends and family. "If I'm feeling a bit homesick, I just look through that," she says.

For Rachel, the worst part of being in S Club 7 is all the travelling which means missing family and friends. She looks back to the time when the S Clubs went to South East Asia and followed this up with a two month filming schedule in LA. "By the time we went off to do the WWF projects, I was so homesick and just wanted to go home." However, the rumour of her leaving because of this is strongly denied. "It is difficult, but I make sure I keep in touch by phone all the time...Friends and family are the most important people in life, in this job you really have to make time to work on relationships."

So, how do her friends react to her success? "They've all been really supportive. They're not jealous at all. I make an effort not to go on about what I've been doing, I'd much rather hear about their lives!" Not surprisingly, Rachel's mobile phone is an essential travelling item and one thing she would hate to be without. "There's nothing better than catching up with friends in a quick break when you're really missing them." Consequently, Rachel admits her phone bill is of huge proportions!

Like the rest of S Club 7, Rachel is committed to various causes. Her chosen endangered animal to support with the WWF is the Siberian Tiger. In *S Club 7 Go*

Wild!, Rachel travelled to the harsh landscape of Far East Russia to find the world's largest cat. "The experience was brilliant, actually seeing the tiger and knowing I was helping to raise awareness about how endangered they are." Rachel wasn't so keen however on the WWF trip she took to Kenya with Paul to see the Black Rhino. "The temperature here was unbearable and I kept getting bitten and then found cockroaches under my bed!"

Musically speaking

Undoubtedly one of the highlights of 2000 for Rachel was seeing *Never Had A Dream Come True* reach number one, particularly as it was for Children in Need. "We followed up the news with a huge party with all our mates," she says. The song is actually a particular favourite of Rachel's, "It has such a beautiful melody, it makes you want to sing along every time."

Another of Rachel's favourites on the album 7 is Natural. "I love the funky feel, it's more of an R&B (rhythm and blues) song. The dancing for it is technically quite demanding, but it works really well...Though of course, one of the main reasons I like it is that I sing the main vocals!"

Looking to the future, Rachel sees herself with a couple of children. She has said she'd ideally like a boy first and then a girl. But that's not planned until she's in her late twenties, so don't fear, S Club 7 is safe!

Were S Club ever to split, Rachel has said she would consider a solo career, maybe picking up on her love of R&B. She'd also love to make movies. There's certainly no lack of determination and ambition in Rachel.